KEELY A

D0447846

by Jane Martin

SAMUEL FRENCH, INC.

45 WEST 25TH STREET   NEW YORK 10010
7623 SUNSET BOULEVARD HOLLYWOOD 90046
LONDON   TORONTO

IMPORTANT BILLING AND CREDIT REQUIREMENTS

Keely and Du was given its professional world premiere at Actors Theatre of Louisville during the 17th annual Humana Festival of New American Plays, March 1993.

In the cast were:

Du .... Anne Pitoniak
Walter .... Bob Burrus
Keely....................................... Julie Boyd
Cole .... J. Ed Araiza
Prison Guard....................... Janice O'Rourke
Orderlies ....Jeremy Brisiel, Jennifer
Carta, Jeff Sexton

Directed by Jon Jory
Scenery designed by Paul Owen
Costumes designed by Laura Patterson
Lighting designed by Marcus Dilliard
Stage Manager, Paul Mills Holmes
Assistant Stage Manager, Emily Fox

CHARACTERS

DU
WALTER
KEELY
COLE
PRISON GUARD
ORDERLIES

TIME & PLACE

Working-class neighborhood, Providence, R.I.

Present.

PRODUCTION NOTE

Keely and Du is written to be played without an intermission. In production, it runs ninety-five minutes. If an act break is required, it should fall at the end of Scene 13.

No scene change, except the last, took more than fifteen seconds with two people assisting. The bed can be held in place by drop bolts and, when removed, along with the water heater, knee-high fridge, stool and chair in the last change, it took thirty-five seconds.

The author recommends that *no* pre-show or between-scene music be used. The only sound cue should be that of an ambulance siren to cover the change from basement to prison.

MUSIC NOTE

CAUTION: Professionals and amateurs are hereby warned that live stage performance rights for the song K-K-K-KATY by Geoffrey O'Hara are controlled exclusively by EMI Feist Catalog, Inc., 810 7th Ave., 36th fl., New York, NY 10019 Attn: David Wolfson. Royalty arrangements and licenses must be secured well in advance of presentation by anyone choosing to perform this song in the play.

KEELY AND DU

An unfinished basement in a working-class home in Providence, RI. Architectural details are meager; a few pipes, a water heater, a cement floor with a drain. There is an old cast-iron bed bolted to the floor, a small box refrigerator, a rocking chair and a stool. The only door has been framed with sheet metal with a viewing slot added. Beside the door is a speaker monitor. On the other side is an electronic keypad used to control access and egress from the inside by inserting a five-number code. In the room a sixty-five-year-old WOMAN is finishing making the bed. SHE wears a housedress. The time is now.

DU. (*Singing absently, her mind elsewhere.*) "K-K-K-Katy, beautiful Katy, you're the only da-da-da-da that I adore, and when the m-moonshine falls on the cowshed, I'll be waiting by the ... " (*SHE finishes the bed and puts two pillows on it from the rocker. SHE starts the song again.*) "K-K-K-Katy, beautiful lady ..."

(*The BUZZER rings through the speaker monitor. DU moves to it and presses the button.*)

DU. Yes?
WALTER. (*On the speaker.*) She's here.

(DU stands lost in thought for a moment.)

WALTER. Hello. She's here.
DU. Yes.

(SHE pulls back the bedclothes neatly. WALTER enters. HE is a man of fifty, neatly dressed in inexpensive slacks, sport shirt and jacket. HE wears a mask. HE carries a suitcase which HE places by the rocker. DU laughs.)

WALTER. I know. I know. (*HE looks over the room.*) You need to put yours on.
DU. (*Crosses to ger her mask.*) I hope she's not allergic. I scrubbed, but ... (*SHE gestures helplessly.*) Old basements ... uh ...you see.
WALTER. It's fine.

(SHE puts on her mask. HE moves to the door and speaks out it.)

WALTER. Now, please.

(HE re-enters. Moments later TWO MEN bring in a hospital gurney. On it is a young WOMAN, early thirties, strapped in. SHE wears a hospital gown. SHE is unconscious. Over the foot of the gurney is a dress and, on it, shoes.)

DU. (*Involuntarily.*) Oh, my.

(The TWO MEN wear jeans and T-shirts or short sleeves. One is young; one isn't. THEY pull the gurney parallel to the bed and unstrap it. THEY move the young woman onto the bed. ONE places the dress and shoes in the suitcase by the rocker.)

WALTER. Thank you. (*ONE nods, neither speak.*) Please be at dispersal in twenty-three minutes, we are running seven minutes late. (*The TWO MEN look at their watches.*) Seven twenty-two.

(ONE adjusts his watch. THEY take the gurney out and close the door.)

WALTER. (*Speaks to Du.*) Is there anything needed?
DU. (*Stands over the young woman, looking down.*) I don't think so.
WALTER. The anesthesiologist says she might sleep through or she might not.

(DU stands looking at her.)

WALTER. I'll be back in four days. Someone will be upstairs. It went very smoothly and cleanly; we have no reason to be apprehensive. (*HE puts down the small suitcase HE carries.*) Everything is here. Your husband wishes you well. Please memorize this. (*HE hands her a slip of paper.*) Only in an emergency. (*HE takes it back. HE takes both her hands in his.*) God be with you.
DU. (*SHE smiles.*) Yes.

(HE suddenly leans forward and kisses her cheek. DU is surprised.)

WALTER. We will prevail.
DU. I know.

(HE goes out the door and closes it. DU inserts locking code into the keypad. A pause.)

DU. We're fine. *(The viewing slot closes. DU turns, moves to the bed and takes the young woman's pulse. SHE moves to the suitcase and opens it, taking out a fairly thick file folder. SHE thumbs through it. SHE finds what she is look for.)* Right handed. *(SHE puts the folder in the bag and takes out a pair of chromed handcuffs. SHE goes to the bed, handcuffs KEELY's left hand and clicks the other cuff on the metal headboard. SHE makes sure this arrangement is comfortable for Keely. Now DU folds the clothes she has removed from Keely and places them back in the bag and re-zips it. DU goes to the bed and takes Keely's pulse. Finished, SHE goes and checks the door and then moves to the rocker, where SHE sits watching the bed and its occupant. SHE sings "K-K-K-Katy, K-K-K-Katy ..." The LIGHTS go down.)*

Scene 2

LIGHTS almost immediately up.
KEELY is moving.

DU. (*Experimentally.*) Keely? (*KEELY moves.*) Keely?
KEELY. Ummmm.
DU. It's alright, honey. Keely? You're alright, you're
just waking up. (*Nothing from the bed. DU sits a moment.
SHE takes off her mask, thinks, puts it back on.*) Keely?
(*Takes the mask off, moves to the suitcase and puts the
mask in it. Crosses to the bed.*) Keely, I'm a friend, I am.
You're just waking up. You're not hurt in any way. You're
in bed, and I'm here to help you.
KEELY. (*Struggling toward consciousness.*) What?
DU. Nothing's wrong with you, you're just waking up.
KEELY. Who were they?
DU. Who, Keely?
KEELY. On the street?
DU. Good people who wanted to help.
KEELY. I feel nauseous.
DU. That's perfectly normal. Try not to move quickly.
KEELY. Thirsty.
DU. I'll get you some water. (*SHE goes to the large
thermos with spigot.*)
KEELY. Hospital.
DU. (*Returning.*) What, honey?
KEELY. Those people ... I'm so foggy ... where is
this?
DU. Is it a hospital, well, no, it's not.
KEELY. I don't know you.
DU. Well, I'm easy to know. (*KEELY drinks.*) Not too
much now. (*SHE takes the cup.*)
KEELY. Thank you.
DU. You're welcome.
KEELY. Dried out. (*Now aware her left arm can't
move.*) Wait ...

DU. I'll just come sit down with you ...

KEELY. What ...

DU. Right here.

KEELY. Hey ... (*Pulls arm against restraint.*) Hey ...
(*SHE twists to try to look at the arm.*) What, what is that?

DU. Don't worry, Keely.

KEELY. Hey! What is this? Who are you? Get me out
of this, you, whoever you are ... please ... where am I?

DU. It's for your own safety ... I'll tell you, but we
should ...

KEELY. Now! Take this off me!

DU. I can't ...

KEELY. Take it off, it's hurting me ... take it off me!

DU. I'm your friend, Keely.

KEELY. I feel sick, I don't feel right. This is ... I'll
start screaming ... it's cutting my wrist ... not right ...
take this off.

DU. You'll hurt yourself ...

KEELY. Now! (*A bloodcurdling scream.*)

DU. Stop it.

KEELY. Help me! Help! Help me!! (*SHE glares at Du.
SHE twists and fights until SHE falls off the bed.*) What
the hell did I do to you? Hahh? Please. Let me go!

DU. You need to calm yourself, honey.

KEELY. Help! Laura! Help me! (*To Du.*) Who are you?
This hurts, it's hurting me. Ow. Ow, ow. I can't stand
this. (*SHE's on her feet, yanking the cuffs, grabbing with
her free hand. SHE tries to drag the bed. SHE tries to tip it
over. SHE starts to cry out of frustration. SHE tries to go
after Du, yelling:*) Let me go! You better let me go!

DU. Please don't hurt yourself.

KEELY. Get these off. My dad's alone. He has to be fed. Do you understand that? He can't move, do you hear me? Come on, what are you doing? Tell me? What do you want me for? Who do you think I am? I'm not anybody; why would you do this? Let me go! This thing is tearing my wrist. I want this off me. Come on, I'm not kidding. Listen, I got seventy bucks in the bank, I can't get laid off. I got two jobs; what time is it? I have to go home, don't you understand me? (*Her diatribe becomes less and less controlled, builds to a peak and then declines into a beaten, exhausted silence that leaves her staring at DU, who sits in the rocker.*) Get this off me. I can't do this. Help! Let me out! Get me out of this. Do you hear me, are you deaf, or what are you, lady? Help! Help! Help me, help me, help me! (*SHE screams in rage and frustration.*) Let me go. What are you? Help! Come on. Come on! Tell me what you want. Tell me what you want! Please. Come on. Help! Please, talk to me, talk to me. Please. Please. (*SHE stands, sweat pouring down her face, her voice hoarse, panting. SHE yanks against the cuff. SHE stands staring at Du. The LIGHTS fade.*)

Scene 3

LIGHTS up. KEELY lies sleeping. An outside LOCK turns. DU enters with a bucket of water, a towel, washcloth and sponge. SHE puts the towel on the stool and the bucket on the floor. KEELY sits bolt upright, startled. SHE stares at Du.

DU. Rise and shine, the British are coming. In the army my husband had a sergeant used to say that every six A.M.! Heavens. Well ... would you like to wash up, Keely? I hoped we'd have a shower, but something about the pipes. (*KEELY doesn't respond.*) Are you a bath person or a shower person? I was bath, but I changed over when I got so that I didn't like looking at myself. You're so aware of yourself in a bath, don't you think? Did you sleep at all? Heavens, I don't see how you could, I really don't.

(*DU reaches out to touch Keely's shoulder, but SHE turns away.*)

DU. Keely?
KEELY. Get away from me!
DU. I can do that, yes. Keely ...
KEELY. Don't talk to me!
DU. I thought you might want to wash yourself.
KEELY. You heard me!
DU. (*Sits in rocker.*) You can tell me if you change your mind.

(*KEELY doesn't move. The LIGHTS fade.*)

Scene 4

In the DARK, a TRAY falls. LIGHTS up. Keely has knocked a breakfast tray presented by Du to the floor.

DU. (*Looking down.*) Well, honey, what is that? What does that mean? I would like you to keep my arthritis in mind when I'm on my hands and knees cleaning that up.

KEELY. (*Eyes flaming.*) I'll keep it in mind.

DU. You need to eat.

KEELY. I'm not eating.

DU. Then they'll feed you intravenously. Well, I'm upset if that's satisfying, I'm not cleaning this up now. (*SHE sits in the rocker. SHE waits. KEELY will not respond.*) No ma'am. No ma'am. Well, not everyone likes 'em scrambled. My middle son, he was poached, and he's still poached if you ask me. That boy was, is and will be a trial. It was his born nature and his grown nature, I swear I had no effect, but that child can make you laugh! Lordy. From this high. Three boys, and lived to tell the tale. Every single one of them on the basketball team, and if that's not the dumbest human activity the mind could come up with, I don't know what is. Run one way, put it in a hole, run the other way, put it in a hole. Lord have mercy. (*No response.*) You can talk or not talk. You'll be here almost five months, here in this room with me. How will we pass the time? You have a special burden, I believe that. I would lift it from you if I could. You are not what I would have chosen, but ... wiser heads. What we think is not everything in this world. You'll be having a baby; perhaps we should start from there.

(*LIGHTS down.*)

Scene 5

*In the DARKNESS we hear a BUZZER. WALTER, on the
speaker: "I will be coming down." LIGHTS up. DU
moves to the door, pushes the speaker's button, and
says:*

DU. Yes. Good. (*SHE turns to Keely.*) I hope you
aren't so angry that you can't listen because it would be
important to listen now. Keely? He is blunt spoken
sometimes, and he is a man, don't let that close your heart.
Keely?

*(DU goes to the suitcase and puts on her mask. There is a
light KNOCK on the door. SHE goes to it and unlocks
it. SHE opens the door. A MAN wearing a mask,
dressed in a suit and tie enters with a briefcase. HE
speaks to Du.)*

WALTER. Good morning, sister.
DU. Good morning.
WALTER. Good morning, Keely. (*No answer. HE goes
to the rocker and pulls it closer to Keely but still beyond
her reach.*) Nana is taking fine care of you, I'm sure. (*HE
looks at the tray on the floor.*) I see you've had your
breakfast. You seem alert and well. The anesthetic we used,
100 milligrams Ketamine, is very mild and will not harm
the baby, we're very sure of that. I know you have other
concerns. Funds have been arranged for your father's care. I
wanted to reassure you. (*A pause.*) Will you talk to me at
this point, Keely, or shall I just talk to you? I know this
must be hard to take in.

KEELY. Who are you?

WALTER. I am a member, Keely, of Operation Retrieval. We are a group of like-minded Christians motivated by a belief in the sanctity of life and the rights of unborn children.

(KEELY puts her head in her hand.)

WALTER. Now, Keely, western man has firmly held to life-supportive principles as promoted by Hippocrates from 450 B.C. until the turn of the century. Since then, certain groups and individuals have been promoting death as a solution to social problems. I do not condone that. You are almost three month's pregnant, Keely.

KEELY. I was raped.

WALTER. You were, Keely, and I find that horrifying. That a man you knew and cared for ...

KEELY. Wait a minute; wait a minute.

WALTER. You are the injured party ...

KEELY. Yeah, right ...

WALTER. In God's eye, and in ours ...

KEELY. And handcuffed, and kidnapped.

WALTER. ... but your unborn child is separate from that issue.

KEELY. No, it isn't.

WALTER. It is a separate life which may not be taken to solve your very real problems.

KEELY. Hey, it's cells, little cells.

WALTER. (*Very clearly.*) It is a separate life.

KEELY. And what about my life?

WALTER. I need to clarify the situation for you ...

KEELY. (*Pulling on her restraint.*) Oh, it's clarified.

WALTER. Keely, there are 1,500,000 abortion deaths on this planet each year, and that is spiritually unbearable. Now, you are one of four young women, geographically distributed, all with child, all seeking abortion, who have been taken into protective custody. Each of you sought out a clinic for different reasons and in different situations. There is, of course, a political dimension here. We chose you as a rape victim, Keely. Rape has always been understood as the extreme edge of abortion policy, and we must make clear that infant rights extend even into this catastrophic area. The rape victim must be given support on every level, but the fact of the child is critical. If medically we must lose or severely harm mother or child, we must choose. If both can survive, both must survive. We intend to document and assist these children's lives, which would otherwise have been lost.

KEELY. What do you mean, document?

WALTER. Document, Keely. We'll discuss it later.

KEELY. Who the hell are you? Screw you people. I'm not a goddamn teenager. You're not God. I want an abortion!

WALTER. Keely …

KEELY. What do you want from me?!

WALTER. We want you to hold your baby. We will care for you here until the seventh month of your pregnancy and then return you home for the birth in the best medical circumstances.

KEELY. Oh, man.

WALTER. We assume the following responsibilities: all expenses relating to the birth of your child will be taken care of, adoptive parents eager to raise the child and capable of so doing will be in touch with you, should you decide to raise your child ...

KEELY. How the hell do you think I'm going to do that, huh? You knew I was pregnant, you knew I was raped, do you know I take care of my dad? Do you know he's paralyzed? Do you know I hold his bedpan? Is that part of what you know? Do you know I work two jobs? Do you know what they are?

WALTER. A child-care subsidy will be provided for the first two years, and there will be an education fund ...

KEELY. What is your name? What ... what ... who are you?

WALTER. You're going to be famous, Keely. You're going to be a famous American. There will be many opportunities open to you and your child. This is difficult for you to understand, but your life has already changed for the better ... (*KEELY laughs.*) I know it's ironic. Are the handcuffs hurting you?

KEELY. Yes.

WALTER. I'm sure there is something we can do. Everything I know about you, Keely, and I know considerable, leads me to believe you will fall in love with your baby.

KEELY. My sister-in-law, she threw her baby on the floor. You think "in love with your baby ..." is all that's out there?

WALTER. It's what should be out there. You are in your third month, Keely. Your baby is sensitive to the touch. If you stroke its palm, it will make a fist.

KEELY. You're going to prison, mister. I'll put you there.

WALTER. You may send me to prison ... (*HE gestures toward Du.*) ... we are both prepared for that spiritually and practically. We have committed our lives. What can I say to you? I am a father, and caring for, learning from my children ... well, you wouldn't understand. They resurrected my life through our Lord Jesus Christ.

DU. She's exhausted.

WALTER. Keely, the abortion procedure you were seeking Wednesday morning is called Suction Curettage. A powerful suction tube is inserted through the cervix into the womb. The baby's body and the placenta are torn to pieces and sucked into a jar. The baby's head is crushed and then extracted.

KEELY. Screw off.

WALTER. It's sometimes hard to recognize a friend at first, Keely, we need direction sometimes, we need people to tell us what to do when we act out of panic or confusion. I have limited your options and taken control to give you the chance to step outside your runaway emotions. I will return your options to you when you are thinking clearly and ready for them.

KEELY. (*Indicating Du.*) She took off her mask, I'll remember her.

(*WALTER looks at Du. A pause, and then HE takes off his mask.*)

WALTER. There, now you've seen us both. Hello.

(*KEELY doesn't reply. DU takes off her mask. WALTER looks at her again briefly. HE rises and moves to the door.*)

WALTER. I am a pastor if you wish counseling about your rape or your pregnancy. One of our doctors will visit you weekly. This lady is a registered nurse. (*A pause.*) You could be my daughter, Keely, and if you were I would do this for you. I'll see about the handcuffs. Goodbye, Keely. (*HE exits, closing the door behind him.*)

DU. (*Goes to the door and locks it. Turning back, SHE cleans up the breakfast.*) I'm sorry they chose you.

(*LIGHTS out.*)

Scene 6

A TRAY crashes in the DARK. LIGHTS up. DU stands over another fallen breakfast.

DU. (*Looking down.*) My husband can eat the same breakfast one hundred times in a row. Goes the same route in the car to the same places. Buys the same color socks by the gross. He is very set in his ways. (*SHE kneels down and cleans up.*) Please talk to me. (*A pause.*) Please talk to me. (*A pause.*) My husband isn't much of a talker. Well, are they ever? To us? I don't know. Oh, about some things. Not about others. I never could understand it. (*SHE pauses. KEELY doesn't reply.*) Now, Keely, truly, are we going to sit here like this? You talked to him; am I so much worse? Well, he's a good man if he doesn't sound like one. The language you use? Honestly. You know what he says where another man would swear? Flub-a-dub-a-dub! Right out in public. Flub-a-dub-a-dub. (*SHE laughs.*)

KEELY. Why should I talk to you? (*Referring to the cuffs.*) Look at this. Why the hell should I talk to you?

DU. (*SHE has finished cleaning. SHE looks at Keely.*) Because you have a life to lead, young lady. That is why "the hell" we should talk. And don't play Miss Self-righteous with me, this is beyond that. None of this is going away, Keely. Deal with it. (*KEELY stares at her, furious.*) Foolishness.

(*LIGHTS out.*)

Scene 7

The LIGHTS come up on WALTER talking to KEELY at the bed. SHE has her hands over her ears. DU stands somewhere above the bed.

WALTER. By twenty-five days, the developing heart starts beating; by forty-five days, it has eyes, ears, mouth, kidneys, liver; it has a brain and a heart pumping blood it has made itself. I know you can hear me, Keely.

KEELY. No.

WALTER. Three months, right now, there is sexual differentiation. The baby sleeps and wakes and excretes and has vocal cords he even tries to use.

KEELY. You have no idea … no idea …

WALTER. At four months … it has eyelashes and expressions you could recognize from your grandmother.

KEELY. Please stop talking.

WALTER. Why wouldn't you let the baby live, Keely? You never have to see it again if that's what you want.

KEELY. No.

WALTER. The baby isn't rape, Keely, the baby is a baby ...

KEELY. Please ... (*SHE starts to cry.*)

WALTER. Last year there were 700,000 people wanting babies who couldn't get them ... listen to me...

KEELY. Don't touch me.

WALTER. I know carrying this baby is difficult and emotional ... but, after abortion there are frightening side effects.

KEELY. Please ...

WALTER. ... serious depression, terrible guilt, mental illness, self-destructiveness.

DU. That's enough.

WALTER. Spare yourself, Keely, finish this in a life-giving way so you can respect yourself.

KEELY. Screw you!

WALTER. (*Forcibly turning her face to his.*) Your mouth should be washed out with soap.

DU. That's enough!

WALTER. (*To Du.*) What are you doing?

DU. I am suggesting that she isn't hearing you ...

WALTER. Yes?

DU. They are important things, and we would want her to hear them.

WALTER. (*Coming back to himself. Understanding.*) Yes.

DU. That's all I'm saying.

WALTER. Thank you.

DU. That's all I'm saying.

WALTER. Sometimes I don't realize ... sometimes I am over-emphatic. (*To Keely.*) Please accept my apologies. (*HE lightly touches Keely's arm.*) That certainly won't happen again. (*SHE stares at him.*) I, umm ... I'll be back this evening.

DU. I didn't ...

WALTER. Is there anything I can bring you? (*No answer.*) Well, then ... (*HE goes and collects his things. To Du.*) Thank you for pointing out that I had overstepped myself.

DU. I just ...

WALTER. I'm sorry, Keely.

(*No answer. HE leaves and closes the door.*)

DU. (*SHE goes to the door and locks it. SHE comes back and sits on the edge of the bed.*) I'll just be here. I won't touch you. I won't say anything. I'd just like to sit here.

(*LIGHTS down.*)

Scene 8

LIGHTS up. DU is mopping the floor.

DU. ... so, the stock market crashed, three days later, there I was. The doctor asked my father what they planned on calling me ... "Calamity Jane," he said. There were ten kids, I was the fourth. Would you like me to stop talking? (*KEELY shakes her head "no."*) My mother, Jesus watch over her, died of leukemia at thirty-seven, leaving ten children, God help us, you can imagine. Well, God provides. I took care of the little ones, and my sister, 'til college took care of me. So much to learn, such a stupid little girl. Thousands of meals I put together. Sometimes I would step into a closet for the peace and quiet. Oh, mercy! Oh, my father was quiet, Lord he was silence in shoes, I mean it ... so tall ... he wore one suit, and he would move through the mess and noise and contention and tears, and he would pick up the fallen, dry the ones who were wet, find the lost and admonish the fallen away with an old wooden spoon. And then he'd go and sit in the midst of the madhouse and read his Bible. When his eyes tired he'd have me read it, on the floor beside him, one hand on my shoulder. You know, I remember a hundred things he did and nothing of what he said. He died of throat cancer, and he died so hard I don't even like to think about it. (*A pause.*) What about your father? (*A pause.*) What about your father? (*Irritation.*) I think you're spoiled rotten, what do you think? You care for your father, and you think that's hard? It's a privilege to do that, young lady. You work two jobs and think you're put upon? There are millions suffering because they can't provide. Your husband forced himself on you? You should have gone to the police. You want to end the life of the baby you are carrying? It's contrary to God's will, it's murder, it's not necessary, it's as selfish an act as you could conceive, and we will not allow you to harm that child or yourself. You are better than that, you know you are, and how you feel or what trouble you might have is not so important as a life.

Now grow up and talk to me. (*A pause.*) What about your father?

KEELY. My father? He can move his right arm and the right side of his face.

DU. I'm sorry.

KEELY. He's a cop who got shot being held as a shield during a drug bust. You mess with a cop's daughter, they will skin you alive.

DU. I am truly sorry.

KEELY. You know what you get for kidnapping?

DU. Well, not to the year I don't.

KEELY. All you've got left. All of your life.

DU. I'm a Bible Christian, Keely, and you can have my life to stop the slaughter is my perspective, I suppose. Not that I could take the prison, Lord, I don't even like low ceilings. I don't know what I'd do. But … Isaiah 44:24, "This is what the Lord says—your Redeemer who formed you in the womb: See, I set before you today life and prosperity, death and destruction, now choose life, so that you and your children may live." (*A pause.*) I don't know if you care anything about the Bible.

KEELY. (*Flaring.*) Hey, I didn't choose to have this baby.

DU. And the baby didn't choose, honey, but the baby's there.

KEELY. And I'm here. I don't have, you know, Bible reading to hold up. I'm not some lawyer, alright, with this argument, that argument, put in this clause, fix the world. I can't do this, take care of my dad, get myself straight, take on a baby, I got, you know, nightmares, stuff like that, I see, whatsername, Princess Di, on some supermarket magazine, I'm there crying, they have to call the manager, because what we've got here, I could get messed up, who knows, killed by who impregnated me, not to mention I might, I don't know, hate this baby, hurt this baby, throw the baby or something like that, I'm not kidding, what's inside me. Now, do you have some Bible quotes for that, or am I just beside the point, handcuffed to this bed, carrying the results of being fucked by my ex-husband while he banged my head off a hardwood floor to shut me up.

DU. I'm sorry.

KEELY. You're sorry?

DU. That was the act of an animal at that time.

KEELY. At that time? You don't know who he was, who he is. Many times. You don't know who I am, and God knows you don't care, with your scrambled eggs and your grandma act, either let me out of here or leave me alone, do you understand me? I wouldn't eat I don't know what if it came from your hands, I wouldn't touch it, I wouldn't let it inside me. You're filth. I don't care what church you come from or who your God is. You're criminal filth, and I will see to it you get yours. Now, leave me alone. (*SHE turns away. There is silence.*)

DU. I can't leave you alone, honey. Nobody wants to be left alone. Not really.

(The LIGHTS fade.)

Scene 9

*The LIGHT comes up on WALTER sitting by Keely's bed
taking things out of a grocery bag beside him on the
floor.*

WALTER. Feeling the baby move. I've always thought
it must be the most extraordinary sensation. Mouth wash. I
believe peppermint was required. Oranges, I hope they're
ripe. It wasn't apples, was it? (*DU nods that it was.*) I'm
not an expert shopper, if you hadn't noticed. Emery boards.
Kleenex. Catsup. And the, uh ... (*Small hangers with
panties.*)
    DU. ... underthings. Size 7 if I'm not mistaken.
    WALTER. (*Nods.*) Now ... (*Takes books out.*) "The
First Year of Life," very informative ... (*Another.*) Doctor
Spock, of course. Proof you can't spoil good advice with
bad politics, and this, on pregnancy, my wife suggested.
(*KEELY doesn't look up.*) Do you know that I love you,
Keely? I love and understand your resistance. I am very
proud of you, oddly enough. You believe you are right, and
you stick to it. If you were swayed by reason or found new
understanding, I believe you would have the guts to admit
it. (*No response.*) Listen to me. You have life inside you.
It perceives. It now recognizes your voice. Your voice
among all others. It cannot be dismissed by calling it a
fetus. (*HE waits.*) The child is separate from how it was
conceived and must also be considered separately from you.
I have no wish to choose between you, but if I must I
choose the child who has no earthly advocate. I can love
you, but I must protect the child. This is my
responsibility. Keely. Keely? You *will* have the child,

Keely, so the book on pregnancy, at least, will be of practical value to you. (*HE puts that book on the bed. KEELY doesn't look up.*) This is a pamphlet on abortion. (*HE opens it.*) Please look at the picture, Keely. (*Again.*) Please look at the picture, Keely. (*SHE doesn't.*) If you cannot look at these photographs, Keely, you have no right to your opinions. You know that's true. (*SHE looks up.*) This. (*HE turns the page.*) This. And this. This. This. This.

(The LIGHTS go down.)

Scene 10

LIGHTS up immediately. DU is in the chair by the bed. SHE takes a pair of baby shoes out of her purse. SHE puts one in the palm of her hand and holds it out to Keely. KEELY looks. SHE takes it. SHE smells it. LIGHTS out.

Scene 11

LIGHTS up on KEELY and DU. THEY sit silently. The time stretches out to almost a full minute.

KEELY. (*Finally.*) I'm hungry.
DU. (*Rising.*) I'll get you some breakfast.

(LIGHTS out.)

Scene 12

KEELY sleeps. DU dozes in the rocker. WALTER enters.
DU wakes as the door CLICKS behind him.

DU. (*Startled.*) What is it?
WALTER. Shhhh.
DU. What? What time?

(THEY converse quietly, aware of Keely.)

WALTER. A little after midnight.
DU. Something's wrong.
WALTER. Not at all. I brought you a milkshake. I just got here from Baton Rouge. A note from your husband. (*HE hands her a folded sheet of lined paper.*) Your husband's been injured. It's not serious.
DU. What?
WALTER. Du, nothing, read it. He broke a finger in a fall.
DU. A fall?
WALTER. They rushed a clinic. He was right in the front where they told him not to be. I'm a little tired.
DU. He's too old for the clinics. It could have been his hip.
WALTER. He wants to be with the children who protest. He doesn't want them to be afraid.
DU. He's seventy years old. How many times do I have to tell you?

WALTER. You try and stop him.

DU. (*Reading.*) He's arrested.

WALTER. Trespassing. Out tomorrow. Write a letter, we'll get it to him. How is she?

DU. Well, she gets her sleep.

WALTER. And?

DU. She's thinking about it now.

WALTER.(*Nods.*) Split the milkshake with me, I haven't eaten.

DU. Did we close the clinic in Baton Rouge?

WALTER. (*Shakes his head "no."*) They put up a chain link fence. They're still killing twenty-five a day.

DU. (*Brushes hair out of Keely's face.*) Thank God we took her.

WALTER. (*Shakes himself.*) I'm asleep on my feet.

(*The LIGHTS fade.*)

Scene 13

LIGHTS up on KEELY sitting up in bed eating breakfast.

DU. (*SHE watches as KEELY eats around the eggs.*) You ever try catsup?

KEELY. What, on eggs?

DU. Oh, we'd buy this spicy kind by the case, Lone Star Catsup. My brothers would heat up the bottles in boiling water so they could get it out faster.

(*A moment. KEELY pokes at her eggs.*)

KEELY. *(Finally.)* For what?

DU. Eggs, rice, they put it on cantaloupe which like to drove my mother from the house. (*An involuntary smile from KEELY, and then, sensing her complicity, silence.*) So, he left high school, Cole?

KEELY. Listen … (*Having started to say something about the situation, SHE thinks better of it, then her need to talk gets the better of her.*) He took a factory job. He was into cars, he wanted this car. His uncle worked a canning line got him on.

(A pause.)

DU. And?

KEELY. We still went out … off and on. We got in an accident, we were both drunk, I got pretty cut up. My dad's cop pals leaned on him. After that … don't know, lost touch.

(A pause.)

DU. Lost touch.

KEELY. I don't want to get comfortable talking to you.

DU. Keely …

KEELY. Forget it.

DU. Please …

KEELY. I said forget it. (*A long pause.*) I'm going crazy in here. I could chew off my wrist here. That paint smear on the pipe up there, I hate that, you know? This floor. That long crack. Everywhere I look. Wherever I look, it makes me sick. (*SHE tears up.*) Come on, give me a break, will you. I gotta get out of here, I can't do this. (*Mad at herself.*) Damn it.

DU. (*Gently.*) Help us pass the time, Keely. You're not giving up. I know that. (*KEELY looks down.*) You lost touch.

KEELY. Yeah. (*A pause.*) There were guys at school, you know, different crowds ... thirty-seven days, right? (*DU nods.*) I was ... man ... I was, umm, waitressing, actually before he left, down at the Gaslight ... he didn't like me working. I just blew him off. (*A moment.*) If I talk, it's just talk ... only talk, that's all ... because this is shit, what you do to me, worse than that.

DU. Only talk.

KEELY. Because I don't buy this, you tell him I don't buy it.

(DU nods. THEY sit. Then:)

KEELY. So I was at a Tammy Wynette concert, you know, somebody else's choice, and there he was, definitely his choice as I found out, and my date is ... well, forget him, so we got together and it got hot really fast and we ended up getting married, which nobody I knew thought was a good idea, which made me really contrary which is a problem I have ... like up to here ... so, you know, what I said, we got married, plus ... (*Finishing the eggs.*) The catsup's alright.

DU. Oh, it's good.

KEELY. I mean I knew who he was, and I did it anyway. I knew about the drinking, I knew about the temper, I don't know where my head was, in my pants, I guess.

DU. Well, I married a man deemed suitable and that can be another problem. There is only one way a man is revealed, and that is day in and day out. You can know a woman through what she says, but don't try it with a man.

KEELY. Yeah, he had a line. I even knew it was a line.

DU. I'll just take the tray.

KEELY. And I knew he drank. Oh, hey, he down-pedaled it before we got married … way, way down-pedaled. He would drink, say two, two drinks, say that was his limit, take me home, go out pour it down 'til ten in the morning, I found that out.

DU. They talk about drugs, but it's still drinking the majority of it, now I have never been drunk in my life, is that something? I'm often tempted so I'll know what I'm missing, yes ma'am, I've tried the marijuana …

KEELY. Bull.

DU. Oh, I have, and it didn't do a thing for me and that's a fact, and I've been in a men's room which I doubt you have, and I've kissed three men in one day, so don't you think you can lord it over me.

KEELY. You smoked?

DU. Oh, yes. Found the marijuana in my son's sock, sat on his bed, waiting 'til I heard him come in the front door, lit up and let him come on up and find me there doing it. Shocked him down to his drawers I might say … straightened him up in a hurry. That's the one who's an accountant now. All boys. I would have given my heart for a girl baby. (*An awkward pause.*) It's noisy, too many boys in a house.

KEELY. (*A pause.*) Suitable?

DU. What? Oh, suitable. I was keeping company with a slaughterhouse man who could pop your eyes out with his

shirt off, but he was an atheist and a socialist and who
knows what else, and that was one too many for my father
so he ran him off and put me together with a nice German
milkman whose father owned the dairy, if you see my
point. August. His name, not the month. I married him at
nineteen, in 1947, and two months later the dairy went
under, so I got no money and he looked just terrible
undressed. The fact is he was an uninteresting man, but he
got into the storage business and turned out a good
provider. Now, listen close here, we went along 'til he
bored me perfectly silent, if you can imagine, and God
found us pretty late when the kids were gone or near gone,
and when God found that man he turned him into a
firebrand and an orator and a beacon to others, and I fell in
love with him and that bed turned into a lake of flame and I
was, so help me, bored no more, and that's a testimony.
There is change possible where you never hope to find it,
and that is the moral of my story, you can stop listening.

KEELY. Right.

DU. It is. Still nothing to look at but I just close my
eyes. The children kept me in that marriage until it became
a marriage and the love I bore them kept me alive until the
marriage could catch up.

KEELY. So what am I supposed to be? Glad?

DU. Things do change.

KEELY. Yeah, they get worse. He drank more, he got
meaner, he screwed around. My dad got shot, Cole wanted
to move to Arizona because he knew I'd have to take care
of him. I'm waitressing, minimum wage, cashier at a car
wash, seventy hours minimum, he drinks himself out of
his job, real thoughtful, right? The recession came on, we
just fought minute to minute anytime we laid eyes on each

other, I said I wanted a divorce, he hit me, and I left. I was out of there fifteen minutes after he hit me ... I was a crazy, out-of-my-mind lunatic I lived with him all that time. Jesus! What the hell was I thinking of?

DU. It was a marriage, Keely.

KEELY. Yeah. After that, he was all over me. I'd look out the window, he'd be in the back yard. The grocery, the library, when I was hanging up laundry, walk into the same bar when I was on a date. He'd come down to the restaurant, say it was about borrowing money, but he knew I wasn't giving him money, forget that, he just liked me to be scared which is what I figured out. Then it stopped for six months, who knows why, then he came back, sent flowers, left messages, begged me to talk to him for one hour, so I invited him over, you know, my dad was in bed, asleep, I thought we could sit down and let go of it. I thought I could take his hand and say we're clear, we're two different people. You know, some dumb ass idea like that. So I fixed him something to eat, and he brought me this stuffed animal, and we were doing, well, not perfect but alright, and I just touched his arm so he would know it was alright, and he locked onto my hand, and I said "let go now," and he started in ... said he needed ... pulled me in, you know, hard, and I got a hand in his face, and he ... he bit down ... bit down hard, and I ... I don't know, went nuts ... bunch of stuff ... got me down on the floor ... got me down on the floor and raped me. That's how he caught up with our marriage, that's how he changed.

(THEY sit in silence.)

DU. It's in the past, Keely.

KEELY. Well, this isn't. (*A pause.*) You believe God sees you?

DU. I do.

KEELY. He sees you now?

DU. I believe he does. (*A pause.*) Keely? ... Keely? (*No answer.*) Almost time for your birthday.

(A pause.)

KEELY. How do you know that?

DU. Now, Keely, that's the least of what I know, and you know it.

KEELY. From my driver's license.

DU. The man says you can have a cake.

KEELY. The man?

DU. The man in charge.

(A moment.)

KEELY. If I do what, I can have a cake?

DU. Oh, a few pamphlets.

KEELY. I'm not reading that crap. I mean it. Don't you bring it anywhere near me.

DU. You're not afraid of information, are you, honey?

KEELY. You call that information?

DU. Well, there's facts to it.

KEELY. I'm not having a baby. I'm not having it and have somebody adopt it. I'm not having it and keeping it. It won't be. It won't.

(A pause.)

DU. What would you like for your birthday, honey? (*KEELY looks at her.*) Besides that. That's not in my power.

(*A pause. Will Keely speak?*)

KEELY. I would like to get dressed. I never liked being in a nightgown. I don't like my own smell, I know that's crazy. You know how you can smell yourself off your night stuff.

DU. Oh, I can share that. That's something doesn't get a bit better with age, let me tell you.

KEELY. I want a chocolate cake. I want to stand up. I want my hands free, I don't care if it's for ten minutes, one minute. I want to walk into a bathroom. I want to stand up, not bent over on my birthday.

DU. Oh, honey. We only do this because we don't know what else to do. We can't think what else … I don't know, I don't … birthdays when they're little, the looks on those faces … those little hands …

KEELY. Little hands, little faces, you make me sick … Jesus, can you listen to yourself? All this crap about babies. You don't care about this baby, you just want it to be your little … I don't know … your little political something, right, God's little visual aid you can hold up at abortion clinics instead of those pickled miscarriages you usually tote around … hold up, Baby Tia, wasn't that the one you had downtown trying to pass it off like it was aborted? I can't believe you don't make yourself sick … throw up … you make me sick, how do you talk this garbage?

DU. (*A moment.*) I have that dress you had on ... something the worse for wear ... I might get it cleaned ... cleaned for your birthday.

(A moment.)

KEELY. I don't hate babies, if that's what you think.
DU. I know that.
KEELY. What the hell is your name? You can ... you can ... you can give me that for my birthday. I would like to know what the hell to call you when I talk to you!
DU. Du.
KEELY. What?
DU. I get called Du.
KEELY. Du.
DU. Uh-huh.
KEELY. Du what? Du why? Never mind, forget it ... I would like to be free for ten minutes on my birthday.
DU. You might have to read some pamphlets.
KEELY. What the hell happened to you, Du? Do you see where we are? Look at this where you got to. Look at me. You used to be a person sometime, right? You look like one. You sound like one. You see the movie "Alien" where they end up with snakes in their chests? What happened to you?
DU. They tear apart the babies, they poison them with chemicals, and burn them to death with salt solution, they take them out by Caesarian alive and let them die of neglect or strangulation, and then later on these poor women, they cut their wrists or swallow lye, and then they bring them to me because I'm the nurse. Over and over. Over and over. Little hands. Little feet. I've held babies.

I've lost babies. I took my own baby through three heart operations and lost that baby. I need to sleep. That's what happened to me.

KEELY. (*Almost gently.*) I can't raise this baby, Du. I'm so angry and fucked up, I just can't do it. I dream how it happened over and over all the time. I'd be angry at the baby, I think so. I'd hurt the baby sometime and might not even know it, that could happen. If I had a baby, my first one, and I gave it away, I'd just cry all the time, I would. I'm doing this on empty and, if I did that, I would be past empty and I don't know. I have such black moods, it frightens me. The baby would come out of being chained to a bed, you know what I mean. It's not my baby, it's the peoples who made me have it, and I couldn't treat it as my baby, not even if I loved it, I couldn't. He'd come around, see. He wouldn't stay off if I had his baby. He would never, ever in this world leave off me, and I think sometime he'll kill me, that's all I can think. Or hurt the baby, whatever, however in his head he could get me, he would do ... would do it. Really. And I can't have his baby ... uh ... it's just not something I can do ... because I'm about this far, you know ... right up to the edge of it ... right there ... right there. (*A pause.*) So I guess it's me or the baby, so I guess that's crazy, but you don't ... I don't show you ... just how ... how angry I really am. I don't. I don't.

(*A pause. The LIGHTS go down.*)

Scene 14

*DU, wearing a stethoscope, sits on the bed, examining
    Keely.*

DU. Probably just a urinary tract infection, as far as we
can tell, oh, very common, practically nothing. The bladder
is right there in front of the uterus, and it compresses when
the uterus enlarges, so, it may not empty completely and
the urine stagnates, and those bacteria just get after it. You
see? So we need to wash more down there, lots of liquids,
vitamin C ... (*SHE moves the stethoscope.*) Now, there's
the fetal heartbeat, would you like to hear ...

*(KEELY does not signify. DU puts the stethoscope on her,
    SHE doesn't resist. DU moves it on her chest.)*

DU. Anything? Anything? Now?

*(KEELY nods. DU lets her listen. SHE does. Suddenly,
    KEELY reaches up and takes off the stethoscope. DU
    takes it.)*

DU. We should get a Doppler probe, you could hear it
better. (*No response.*) Oh, panty liners, I forgot, the
vaginal discharge will be increasing.

(SHE goes to make a note. LIGHTS down.)

Scene 15

*The LIGHTS come up with WALTER and KEELY in
heated argument. DU stands upstage*

KEELY. ... cannot do this!

WALTER. Living in a nation based on ...

KEELY. ... do this to people ...

WALTER. Christian values ...

KEELY. Saving these babies while you rip up the rest
of us ...

WALTER. Because it is a central issue in a Christian
society ...

KEELY. My dad locked in a bed, man, who takes care
of him ...?

WALTER. We address those responsibilities, Keely ...

KEELY. ... like I was some baby farm, baby sow, like
they make veal by nailing those calves' feet to the floor ...

WALTER. Because you will not confront ...

KEELY. ... 'til I'm fattened up for Jesus, right?

WALTER. That's enough, Keely.

KEELY. Enough, my ass!

WALTER. *Do not shout at me!* Christ says in the ...

KEELY. Christ this, Christ that ...

WALTER. Because you will not take responsibility ...

KEELY. So you and a bunch of old guys ...

WALTER. When you have alternatives that clearly ...

KEELY. ... can do whatever you want and ram your
Christ right up my ...

WALTER. Enough! You listen to me, young lady, you
are carrying a child and you will carry it to term. As to my

Christ, he will speak to you, saying "Be fruitful and increase in number and fill the earth ...

KEELY. Yeah, that's really worked out ...

WALTER. "For your lifeblood I will surely demand an accounting. I will demand an accounting from every animal. And from each man, too ...

KEELY. Animals and men, right?

WALTER. "I will demand an accounting for the life of his fellow man.

KEELY. So I must be one of the animals ...

WALTER. " ... For in the image of God has God made man."

(KEELY spits full in his face. WALTER steps back, takes out a handkerchief and wipes his face.)

WALTER. Thank you. I have no right to speak to you in that tone. You are a young woman under enormous and unfortunate stress in a situation beyond your understanding where decisions must be made for you in a gentle and reasonable way. I apologize, it will not happen again.

KEELY. Fuck you.

WALTER. Thank you for accepting my apology.

(Suddenly, both KEELY and DU explode in laughter, it continues, THEY are overwhelmed by it. Slowly, THEY control themselves. It breaks out again. At last, as WALTER watches them, unsmiling, it stops.)

WALTER. You find obscenity amusing?

(A beat. The WOMEN are again overwhelmed by laughter.)

WALTER. We are one nation, under God. And the moral law of our God. (*HE waits for another outburst of laughter.*) ... is all that makes us a nation and within the boundaries of those laws we may speak and decide as a people ... (*One last fit of the giggles.*) ... but when we transgress or ignore Christ's commandments we no longer have democracy, we have anarchy, we no longer have free speech, we have provocation, and this anarchy begins in the family which is a nation within the nation, which sustains and teaches and holds dear these precepts which makes us one. And when that family sunders, and turns on itself, and its children make their own laws and speak only anger, then will the nation founder and become an obscenity that eats its young. (*HE waits a moment and then turns on his heel and leaves, closing the door hard behind him.*)

DU. Oh, my.

KEELY. Oh, my.

WALTER. (*Re-enters, picks up the briefcase he has left.*) We have further business in the morning. (*HE exits again.*)

DU. I shouldn't have laughed, I don't know what I was laughing at.

KEELY. You were laughing because it was funny, Christ doesn't want this.

DU. I don't know.

KEELY. Well, He doesn't. (*SHE throws the pamphlets that have been on the bed on the floor.*) And this stuff is sewage. And I don't want any more hamburgers or catsup or microwaved peas. And I want a woman doctor instead of that dork with a "Turbo-Christian" T-shirt and his icy hands. And how about some trashy magazines, maybe a TV, books with sex scenes, you know, not the disciples and the Last Supper, plus my back hurts, my legs ache, I'm clammy, I'm cramping, and I would like to see Batman VII, or whatever the hell they've got out there, hell, I don't care, take me to traffic school, I'll think I've gone to goddamn heaven!

DU. (*Holds up a key on a key ring.*) Happy birthday.

KEELY. Oh, my God.

DU. (*Tossing it to her.*) Yes, He is, whether you know it or not. (*SHE goes to the half refrigerator.*)

KEELY. (*Trying the cuffs.*) My God, does this open this?

DU. And from the fridge ...

KEELY. What?

DU. (*Taking out the dress Keely was delivered in. It is freshly dry-cleaned, on a hanger, in see-through plastic. SHE holds it up.*) Nice and chilly.

KEELY. Yes!

DU. And one more thing ...

KEELY. (*The handcuff opens.*) Oh, man. Forget the sex. This is ... so cool. I can't believe this.

DU. (*Taking it from behind the heater, a six-pack.*) Warm beer. (*SHE brings it to Keely.*)

KEELY. I can stand up. Whoa, a little ... (*DU moves toward her.*) No, I'm alright. Beer, that's incredible. You don't have any idea. Nobody could have any idea. Standing up straight is this unbelievable pure high.

DU. I couldn't do the cake, I tried, I'm sorry. I could only get out once and I thought the dress was better ... would you have rather had the cake?

KEELY. No, Du, the dress is fine.

DU. I could have gotten the cake.

KEELY. I'll put it on. Just give me a minute.

DU. Okay.

KEELY. Whoa. Walking. Let me give this a try. Oh, man. It feels like weird, you know? Don't let anybody tell you you don't forget how to do it.

DU. Please, please be careful.

KEELY. This is good, Du, this is really, really good.

DU. The beer is hot because I thought if he looked in the ice box I'd rather he found the dress, well, I don't know what I thought, I was so nervous.

KEELY. Hot beer, okay. Maybe I'll give that dress a try, what do you think?

DU. Can I help you?

KEELY. No, actually, Du, I would like to do it by myself, call me crazy, it seems like a real treat. Maybe you could crack the beer or something.

DU. I haven't had a beer in twenty years. On my birthday I would split a Fehrs beer with August.

KEELY. Hard to lift the old arm …

DU. His father would bring it over in his Studebaker. They don't make either one anymore. Those Studebakers. You couldn't tell if they were coming or going.

KEELY. Does the mystery man actually talk or does he just make speeches?

DU. Walter?

KEELY. That guy's name is Walter? (*DU nods.*) Like he was really human? Okay, this is sort of on. Boy. I'm pregnant. I know I'm pregnant now. (*A pause.*) This life is strange, huh? (*A pause.*) I don't care, I'm in a dress. (*A look at Du.*) Thank you.

DU. Happy birthday.

KEELY. I never realized it had that word in it. Am I supposed to drink beer?

DU. (*Taken aback.*) I don't think one is dangerous.

KEELY. (*A moment.*) Could I have the opener?

DU. They twist off.

KEELY. Right. I spit in his face. I can't believe that.

DU. He provoked you.

KEELY. Yeah. (*A moment.*) Whose side are you on?

DU. He is with God, but he is insufferable about it.

KEELY. Yeah.

DU. (*Nods.*) But he is with God.

KEELY. My idea is that after two beers he doesn't exist.

DU. Oh, I think one would be my limit. (*KEELY hands her one.*) Thank you.

KEELY. How do you know I just won't hit you over the head?

DU. Would you? (*No answer.*) Would you do that, Keely? (*No answer.*) Because there are people upstairs. Because you can't bar the door and, after hurting me, you would still be here.

KEELY. (*A moment.*) There are guys upstairs?

DU. Yes.

KEELY. Do they like beer?

DU. They call it the "blood of the beast."

KEELY. Right. (*Looks at her beer.*) To what?

DU. Honey, I think you're the birthday girl.

KEELY. (*Toasting.*) To the next half hour.

(*DU sips. KEELY literally chugs the bottle.*)

DU. My stars! Oh, I wouldn't do that. Keely, have you
lost your senses?

KEELY. I'm trying. (*SHE opens another one.*)

DU. We have all night.

KEELY. And I would like to spend it fucked up,
begging your pardon, blasted, Du, I would really enjoy
that. (*SHE drinks.*) Discount beer, don't knock it.

DU. You might want to sit down for a minute.

KEELY. No way. I forgot I had legs. (*Touching Du's
shoulder.*) I don't want to sit down, okay? Boy, I never met
anybody who would really take it to the limit like you and
that guy. Have an idea or a feeling and just nail that sucker
to the wall. Cole, my ex ... you know ... if you push,
he'll pull, he'll just keep on, but he's crazy ... I don't
think you're crazy, are you? (*SHE drinks.*) Have this idea
about how things should be and take it all the way to here?
All the way to the handcuffs? Never met anybody like that.

DU. You look nice.

KEELY. Yeah, right.

(*DU hands KEELY a pocket mirror.*)

KEELY. Whoa. I don't know about looking in this.

DU. You look nice.

KEELY. Was the kid that died a girl?

(*DU nods. KEELY looks in the mirror.*)

KEELY. Well, that was a mistake. (*SHE looks again.*)
Oh, God. I'm so wormy. No color. Look at this hair.

DU. I could put it up for you.

KEELY. Yeah?

DU. Curl you up the old way like I did for my sisters.

KEELY. How's that?

DU. Rags. Rag it. Yes, rag curls, they always come out nice.

KEELY. God, someone putting up my hair, that's been a long time.

DU. Make you feel better. Toward the end, my mother, nobody at home, but when I ragged her, she'd smile.

KEELY. Okay, if you drink your beer.

DU. Well, I can do that. (*Pats bed.*) You sit down here.

KEELY. Wow, I am already ... plastered.

DU. Now I can't do it standing up. (*SHE goes to her purse.*) I brought a good piece of flannel just in case.

KEELY. I would really like someone to touch me.

DU. (*Holding it up.*) My favorite color. (*KEELY sits.*) I do feel badly about that cake.

KEELY. Forget it. A little dizzy here. Cole wouldn't let me put her out for adoption, not even if I could stand it he wouldn't. (*A pause.*) You actually think you're my friend, don't you? I'm serious. It's a serious question.

DU. Yes.

KEELY. You always chain your friends to a bed?

DU. On her behalf, I would.

KEELY. Funny how there's always been somebody around who knew just what I needed and made me.

DU. Good or bad, depending.

KEELY. Yeah, and they were always men.

DU. Yes, they make a habit of it.

KEELY. I mean all the time. *All* the time.

DU. Sit still.

KEELY. My dad, oh yeah, it was *real* clear to him, my brother, he picked it right up, boyfriends, my husband, my

boss where I work, they got right in there on *my behalf* ...
on my behalf. Hell, I even liked it, I even asked for it. I
even missed it when I got over it and right then, right then
you bastards were back on my behalf once again.

DU. Now, I don't do hair and listen to swear words.

KEELY. No problem, I'd rather have my hair done. Behalf. No kidding. Maybe less than half. Be less than half. I
got the message. You finished that beer yet? (*SHE looks.*)
Two more coming up.

(*SHE gets them, opens them. DU knocks one over.*)

DU. Oh, my.

KEELY. Where's your husband?

DU. Out doing the Lord's work.

KEELY. Like you?

DU. Like me.

KEELY. Nice marriage. (*DU nods.*) Somewhere out
there? (*DU nods.*) Know who else is out there? The FBI,
fed cops, state cops, town cops, dry-cleaners, every living
eye in Cincinnati.

DU. We're not in Cincinnati, honey.

(*A pause.*)

KEELY. Where am I?

DU. Well, you're a long way from Cincinnati.

(*Pause.*)

KEELY. I know your face, bunch of stuff about you.
When I'm one day out, you'll be one day in. I know your
name.

DU. You might. We've been in our Lord's underground
for three years, honey. That other person ... well ...

KEELY. For what?

DU. For lives. Our Lord. For an end to this holocaust.

KEELY. But you don't care what happens to me.

DU. I would give my life for you to be well with a
healthy baby.

KEELY. (*Takes a long pull on her third beer.*) Forget
this. (*SHE exhales, SHE drinks.*) Know what I like to do?
I like to climb. Straight up. Straight, straight up. Colder
than hell. The colder the better. I like the frost on the
eyebrows, you know? (*DU has been working on her hair
for some time.*) That feels good. I used to pull my own
hair, it was like a habit. Fear of heights. I don't have it. I
always thought I would have it, but I don't have it.

DU. Sit still.

KEELY. Cole screwed around with climbing ... when
he was sober. He like kept at me, you know, so I tried it.
The pisser was, I was great ... what can I say, I was, and
did it frost him and did I love it? I could do stuff in rock
shoes without an ice ax he couldn't even get near. It was so
cool. Whip up a crack line, leave him on the wall. This
one guy said I could be a pro, no kidding. Went solo, what
a feeling, man. Cole yelled at me, Dad yelled at me, I
really didn't give a damn, I didn't. Met some people, took a
week off, caught a ride with these two women out to
Fremont Peak in Wyoming. Man, I never saw anything
like that. Make your hair stand up on your neck. They got
these weird sleeping bags you can hang vertically from a

sheer wall and get into? So I'm way, way up, right? And some weather blows through, so I roped myself in and got this hanging bag out and spent the night. I was hanging in this bag, see, 3,000 feet straight down, colder than hell, and I thought, well, you may pee from fear or freeze on the wall, but there is nobody up here to do any goddamn thing on your behalf. I got down from there and got a divorce. Boy, it was a good night's sleep up there, I'll tell you.

DU. Well, you shouldn't do a thing like that by yourself.

KEELY. It was … I don't know what it was.

DU. Turn this way.

KEELY. You ever done anything, like that?

DU. I'm not sure I know what you mean?

KEELY. Done … done anything.

DU. Raised sisters and brothers. Raised three good boys. (*A pause.*) I guess I'm doing something now.

KEELY. Yeah. You're way out there now.

DU. Yes, I suppose I am.

KEELY. Yeah you are. Get me out of here.

DU. I've thought about it.

KEELY. But you would?

DU. I would do for you, Keely, anything I didn't have to do against myself.

KEELY. You do this against me.

DU. No ma'am.

KEELY. You choose the baby's life over my life.

DU. No ma'am. Your life is in your hands. You liked that mountain because you were perfectly alone, Keely, but what I hope and pray for is perfect union and powerful life-giving connection … I long for it, need it, and I'm thinking that if you get your wish and I mine, my spirits will soar, and yours ... well, I can't imagine "perfectly alone," I really can't. A mother can be together with a child in a perfect way, in a union that surpasses any wish you ever wished for yourself. If you haven't felt it, you can't imagine it, and it's within your power to feel it. There is union, they say, with a higher power. The baby though, that's a sure thing, oh, I can guarantee it.

KEELY. I would give all the babies and Gods just to be alone with myself now, I'm sorry but I would. I don't want to be in another box where something else is more important than I am.

DU. There is always something more ...

KEELY. Maybe when I get healthy, but not now. They say an animal will go off by herself to heal. That's what I want.

DU. It's the wrong time, Keely.

KEELY. I haven't ever been alone! Sharing with my brother, moving in with roommates, moving in with Cole, moving back to Dad's, always other people in the room, always hearing other people talk, other people cough, other people sleep. Jesus! I dream about Antarctica, you know, no people, just ice. Nobody on your side of the bed, no do this, don't do that, no guys and what they want, what they have to have, just this flat white, right, as far, you know, as far as you could see, like right out to the edge, no items, no chairs, no cars, no people, and you can listen as hard as you want and you couldn't hear one goddamn thing.

DU. That would be dying, Keely.

KEELY. Yeah? Good. I'll go there then, where you can listen as hard as you want and you can't hear ... whatever ... so, if you wanted to hear something, you would have to hear yourself breathe, like you were in a white sack and there wasn't anything out there. (*A still moment.*) He said, "You want it? You want it? You want it?" Perfect rhythm, you know, banging my head off the floor. And I thought, this is like a beat, you know, had a beat, and I was inside this sound and I looked up and his eyes were completely blank, man, like moons. I almost got his eye. I came real close. I wanted that eye. I wanted it. Well, you don't get everything you want.

DU. Oh, baby.

KEELY. I kind of drifted off while he pumped. Yeah, I was out of there for sure …

DU. No more now.

KEELY. The sleeping bag …

DU. Shhhh.

KEELY. Up there in the sleeping bag …

DU. I know.

KEELY. It was real cold.

DU. I know.

KEELY. Then he went home. Hold me.

DU. Yes.

KEELY. More. Tighter.

DU. I got you. I got you.

KEELY. (*Letting herself be rocked.*) Forget this.

DU. Shhhh.

KEELY. (*Rage, not at Du but at the other.*) Noooooo!!

DU. (*Still rocks her.*) That's right. That's right. It's alright. It's alright. (*SHE sings softly.*) K-K-Katy … beautiful lady … you're the only g-g-girl that I adore …

(The LIGHTS fade out.)

Scene 16

The next morning. KEELY is asleep in Du's arms. DU sleeps as well. The squawk box springs to life.

WALTER'S VOICE. Coming down. (*THEY stir.*) Coming down.
DU. (*Waking.*) Oh, my.

(SHE tries to disengage herself. KEELY wakes.)

WALTER'S VOICE. Coming down.
KEELY. What is it?
DU. The room.
WALTER'S VOICE. Please reply.
KEELY. Quick.

(THEY start to clean the room almost in a panic. DU grabs empty beer bottles and stashes them behind the heater. KEELY shoves the hanger and plastic bag under her mattress.)

WALTER'S VOICE. What is going on?

(DU moves to the microphone. KEELY strips off her dress and puts it under her covers.)

DU. (*Into microphone.*) Come ahead.

(KEELY puts on the nightgown. DU unlocks the cuffs. We hear Walter's KEY in the lock. KEELY gets into

the cuffs and sits on bed. The door opens. DU begins to work on Keely's hair. WALTER enters.)

WALTER. Good morning.
DU. Good morning.
WALTER. What is going on, please?
DU. I'm sorry.

(WALTER doesn't answer, HE simply looks at her.)

DU. Last night was her birthday, I brought her beer as a gift, I didn't answer you because we were hiding the bottles.
WALTER. May I see them, please? (*DU gets the six-pack and holds it up.)* Where are the bottle caps?

(SHE takes them out of her pocket. HE looks at them.)

WALTER. There's one more. (*SHE finds it and hands it to him.*) You used an opener?

(SHE shakes her head "no." HE looks at bed. SHE doesn't respond.)

WALTER. I find this ... unacceptable. (*An outburst.*) What the hell could you have been thinking of? (*HE takes the time to regain control.*) That was stupid and destructive. You broke the discipline that protects us and the work. Alcohol is harmful to the child, which is our primary concern. Worst of all, you've made it impossible for me to trust you. What else were you doing?
DU. I put up her hair.

WALTER. And what else?
DU. I held her until she fell asleep.

(A pause.)

WALTER. Good morning, Keely.
KEELY. Hey.

(A pause.)

WALTER. You may finish her hair.

(HE moves around the room examining it. DU moves to Keely.)

WALTER. Hell is a place, it is not an obscenity. *(KEELY and DU exchange a glance.)* It would be very difficult for two women in this circumstance not to develop complicity. I should know that. *(DU goes on taking the rags out.)* The easy part of this for you, Keely, is that you have been coerced. We have had to coerce you because the laws which should have guided you are made by venal, self-serving politicians who invariably do the easy thing. You will shortly be returned to your home where you will be confronted by hard choices to be made without guidance. You will choose whether to love and raise your child or give the child up to young parents in a functioning and successful marriage who will become that child's family. You won't be coerced, you will choose. I don't need to tell you how difficult single parenting is. You've been kind enough to read the books I provided you. *(DU finishes.)* People who make jokes at the expense of family and

ridicule those of us who understand its central, un-
negotiable worth are contemptible, callow, duplicitous
fools. Believe me, they are the most dangerous people in
this society. If I could teach you one thing, I would teach
you that. (*A moment.*) Cole is here to see you, Keely.

KEELY. Noooo!

WALTER. Listen …

KEELY. Absolutely not! You keep him out of here, do
you hear me? I don't want to see him. I won't see him.

WALTER. Cole is here to see you, you ought to listen
to him.

KEELY. If you bring him in here, I'll kill him, or I'll
kill myself, or I'll kill you if I get anywhere near you.

WALTER. He is changed from the inside out, actually
transfigured, he wants your forgiveness.

KEELY. I'm warning you.

WALTER. You don't believe in forgiveness?

KEELY. Not for him, and you better not bring him in
here.

WALTER. He has accepted Christ into his life. He has
denied stimulants. He has cast out evil and accepted
responsibility. He asked me, Keely, if he might mortify
his flesh, begged me to witness, and in seclusion he lashed
himself until he fainted.

KEELY. Yeah! Well, I wish I'd seen it.

WALTER. This man who has been cleansed is not the
man who attacked you.

KEELY. Goddamn it! Are you, crazy, you are all crazy,
do you know that? You think I care about rapists who find
Jesus? The two of you wailing away in some back room.
He did it to me, and I loathe him in ways you cannot begin

to imagine. Let him hold you down and do it and you might have some idea. Keep him out of here, man!

WALTER. He won't touch you, Keely. I have promised him ten minutes to talk to you.

KEELY. No!

DU. Don't make her.

WALTER. (*Looks at Du and then at Keely.*) I'll give you a moment to compose yourself. (*HE exits.*)

KEELY. Du?

DU. I didn't know.

KEELY. Are you sure?

DU. (*A small pause.*) I knew he was saved.

KEELY. How?

DU. They found him and worked with him.

KEELY. They?

DU. We.

KEELY. So you knew?

DU. (*A pause.*) Yes.

KEELY. He was always going to come here?

DU. It was always possible. (*A pause.*) Let me brush your hair.

KEELY. No, thank you.

(*DU comes and sits on the bed.*)

KEELY. Don't.

DU. Keely …

KEELY. Don't sit on the bed.

DU. (*Gets up.*) If you forgave him, you'd be free of him, don't you think so?

KEELY. I should have put him in jail.

DU. Why didn't you?

(KEELY shakes her head, SHE doesn't know.)

DU. You should have, honey. You gave us a harder time because you didn't. Sometimes you have to revenge before you forgive, but then the only way finally to rid yourself and clean yourself is the forgiveness our Lord makes sacred. It's the only armor.

KEELY. So it's my fault?

DU. I didn't say that, honey.

KEELY. I think you said it's my fault.

DU. I didn't say that. I believe that in extremity you must punish, which is God's wrath, or forgive, which is God's grace.

KEELY. This is from nowhere, this is just talk. You haven't been there, you don't have a clue. There are some things it's your job not to forget. That's God's grace if there is any.

DU. Honey ...

KEELY. I forgive you, you brought me a beer. (*DU moves toward Keely.*) No more.

(It's quiet. WALTER moves back into the room. COLE enters. HE wears a neat blue suit, white shirt and conservative tie. HE has short hair, recently barbered, and carefully shined shoes. HE is serious and, if possible, handsome. HE is, just below the surface, very nervous. The effect is oddly engaging.)

COLE. Hello, Keely. (*No answer. SHE regards him.*) Your dad's well. I see him every day. I brought one flower because I didn't know what else to bring. I got it out of your yard. (*HE puts it at the bottom of the bed and backs away again.*) Are you alright? You look alright. (*HE turns to Walter.*) Does she have to be handcuffed?

(*WALTER nods yes. HE goes out into the hall and brings in a straight-backed chair which HE places for Cole a few feet from the bed. COLE sits in it. WALTER and DU stand.*)

COLE. What I did, it was something an animal would do. I should have been killed for it. I would wake up in the middle of the night and think that. Every night. I couldn't stand to look at myself. I didn't like to look down and see my hands or my feet. I wouldn't use a pen or a pencil because then you have to see your hand. I grew a beard because I couldn't shave. I wore the same clothes all the time, I was up to a quart a day.
KEELY. Save it for Jesus.

(*A long pause.*)

COLE. They found me. I was out. I wasn't human anymore. I won't describe it. Remember when we went down to Pensacola? That was some trip. Hey, I got your cat. I'm taking care of your cat. You got it after, right? I've been wondering what its name is? Your cat. What its name is? It's a great cat. I call it Stripes, you know, because I don't know. (*A long pause.*) I would cut off my hand, you know, like they used to do. I would do that if it would make a difference.
KEELY. Do it.
COLE. (*A moment.*) Okay, Keely.

KEELY. And don't ever use my name. I don't let you. I don't want your mouth on my name. (*A moment.*) You won't cut off your hand, you don't have the balls.

COLE. I could do anything.

WALTER. This isn't what we're here for.

COLE. Anything.

KEELY. To somebody else, you son-of-a-bitch.

WALTER. We are a family here. Like it or not like it. The father, the mother, two children.

KEELY. You're the father here?

WALTER. Effectively. Effectively, Keely. We are a family, because no family exists for either of you. We are a family because there is a child to be considered here. I ensure the child will live and hope to see it thrive. Because I have more experience of life than you, I know that later you will understand the wisdom of this position. Both of you have responsibilities to this child. The acceptance of these responsibilities is not optional in this family. I say that as the head of the family. We are here to discuss how to discharge those responsibilities. I will ensure that we do. (*To Cole*.) Say what you have to say.

COLE. Take me back. Forgive me. I loved you in a bad way, a terrible way, and I sinned against your flesh and spirit. God forgive me. I'm an alcoholic but I don't drink now. I don't know … I was … lived like … didn't know right from wrong, but I'm with Jesus now. I accept Him as my Lord and He leads me in His path. I will stay on the path. I will stay on the path. We were married, Keely, you are carrying my baby, let's start from there. I put you on a pedestal, Keely, I do, I wouldn't say it, and I am in the mud, I'm drowning and I ask you to lift me up and then we minister to this child. Jeez, Keely, our child. You know in my house, in my father's house, Jeez, what were those kids, they were nuthin', they were disposable. In your house, right, you know what a time you had. You know. But it can be different for him. I'm different, look in my eyes, you know that. Hey, my temper, you know, I don't do that, it's over ... (*Indicating Walter.*) Ask him is it over. I think about you every minute, every day. I want to dedicate my life to you, because it's owed, it's owed to you. You got my baby. I hurt you so bad you would kill a baby! That's not you, who would describe you, you would do that? Jeez, Keely, don't kill the baby. I brought a book we could look up names, we could do that tonight. You pick the name, I would be proud. I'm going to wait on you. You're the boss. They got me a job. I'm employed. Five o'clock, I'm coming home. Boom. No arguments. I help with the house, we can be partners. I'm back from the dead. I don't say you should believe me but because the baby you should test me out. You gotta take my hand here, we could start from there, I'm asking you. (*His hand extended, HE waits, a long time.*) Come on, Keely. I love you. I can't make love to another woman, you know what I mean. (*His hand is still out.*) You loved me and I destroyed that out of the bottle. But, Jeez, look at me, took off thirty pounds, I don't care what they tell me at A.A., I'm never taking another drink. I'm never. I wanted to suffer what you suffered so I had them whip me, I wanted to take off the flesh, I wanted more pain. I wanted more pain. I wanted more pain. I wanted your pain. I wanted to be even with you so I could put out my hand and we could be one to one. Come on, take my hand. Come on, Keely. Come on, Keely. (*A time.*) I dream of your body, baby. For all those years I knew the small of your back, it's burned into my hand. I worship your body, I adore you. Come on. Come on. (*HE moves off the chair.*) You don't have to ask me to be on my knees, I'm on my knees. What am I without you? I'm only what I did to you. I can't demand. What could I demand? Choose to lift me up. Who else can you save, Keely, but me? I'm the only one you can save. (*His hand is inches from hers.*) Take my hand, come on. It's five inches, you know what I mean? It's right here. It's right here for us to do. You don't have to make me promises, I'm not saying that. How could I expect that. I'm saying take the hand alone. (*A short wait.*) Let me touch your hand. Don't speak. Don't speak, I'm saying. Let me come this far and touch your hand, okay? Okay? Just the touch. Okay? (*HE touches her hand. SHE doesn't withdraw it.*) Oh, my God. Oh, my God, there is stuff leaving me. Okay, Keely, I thought about a pledge, what I could make to you, if I could touch you. No harm. No harm is what I thought of. Look, I want to turn your hand over, make it palm up, okay? This is make or break, Keely. Right now. Right now. Close your hand, take my hand. You know what I mean? One gesture, you could save me. We could raise a child. With one gesture we could do that. Come on, Keely. Come on, Keely.

(*In an incredibly quick move, KEELY brings his hand to her mouth and sinks her teeth into it.*)

COLE. Ahhhhhh ...

(*HE can't get the hand back, SHE goes deeper.*)

COLE. Ahhhhhhhhhhhhhhhhhhhhh ... (*HE screams. HE puts his other hand on her head and tries to force her off.*) Ahhhhhhh ...

(*WALTER grabs him from behind, but HE has pulled free and slaps her hard. WALTER pulls him back. DU steps in front of him.*)

COLE. God love and forgive you!
WALTER. Idiot!
KEELY. Get out, go on, get out!
COLE. I can see the bone what she did.
WALTER. Come with me.
COLE. (*His fist doubled.*) What she did to me.
WALTER. Submit your will, come with me.
COLE. (*Angrily.*) I love you, Keely!
DU. There's first-aid upstairs.
WALTER. Come on, Cole.
COLE. Jesus, in thy name!
WALTER. Come on, Cole.
DU. I'll take care of him.
WALTER. (*Leading him out.*) This way now. Walk with Jesus, Cole. This way now.

(*WALTER and DU take him out. Without hesitation, KEELY reaches under the mattress and pulls out the wire hanger her dress had hung on. SHE brings it up to her cuffed hand and untwists the hanger, straightening it out. SHE pulls the sheet over herself, puts the wire under the sheet with her free hand and works to abort herself. It goes on. The LIGHTS go down.*)

Scene 17

The LIGHTS come up. It is minutes later. The bed sheet covering KEELY is soaked with fresh blood. KEELY lies still; she has passed out. We hear WALTER speak offstage.)

WALTER'S VOICE. Did we leave it open?

(We don't hear the answer. Moments later, HE steps into the room.)

WALTER. Oh, dear God. (*Over his shoulder, up the stairs.*) Help me! Come down here. (*HE goes to the bed.*) Keely. Keely. (*HE lifts the corner of the sheet. HE drops it. Momentarily HE puts his face in his hands.*) God help us.

(DU enters through the door, sees, comes directly to the bed.)

WALTER. She's aborted.
DU. (*Looks under the sheet; SHE removes the hanger.*) Call the paramedics.
WALTER. I'll try to reach Dr. Bloom.
DU. No. No time. You have to call 911.
WALTER. That's not possible. Where did she get it?
DU. It doesn't matter. I'll call.
WALTER. Think, this is kidnapping.
DU. She's losing blood.

WALTER. I know.

(SHE starts past him; HE stops her.)

WALTER. You have to give me thirty seconds. (*HE walks to the bed and touches Keely.*) We'll clear out. It will take five to seven minutes. We'll call the paramedics from a pay phone.
DU. I'm not leaving her. I'll call.
WALTER. Think.
DU. I don't care.
WALTER. Du.
DU. I won't implicate you. Go on.
WALTER. No.
DU. We're Christians. You're needed, I'm not.
WALTER. No.
DU. There is a larger world, a larger issue. (*SHE goes to Keely.*) I'm getting help, honey, it's coming. I won't be gone two minutes. (*SHE kisses her forehead. SHE moves toward the door, touching Walter.*) God be with you.

(SHE exits. HE stands. HE puts one hand over his eyes for a moment. HE looks at Keely. HE exits. The LIGHTS go down.)

Scene 18

LIGHTS up, the stage is empty except for a straight-backed chair off to one side. A female prison GUARD enters

*and presses a button on a speaker phone located on the
wall.*

GUARD. Code 417-26. Officer Carrington. Requesting
pick-up 9923739 Visitors' Area. Time unit one-half hour.
Over. Doing it now.

*(SHE exits and returns with DU in a wheelchair, dressed in
a bright orange jumpsuit, prison issue. SHE positions
her center. BUZZER sounds. SHE goes to the speaker.)*

GUARD. We're here. No prob.

*(SHE waits a moment. KEELY enters. SHE wears a light
summer dress. SHE carries a string bag filled with
items and a McDonald's breakfast in a bag. The
GUARD moves the other chair opposite Du. KEELY
sits. DU has had a minor stroke and lost the use of her
left hand.)*

GUARD. One-half hour.
KEELY. Hi. Breakfast. *(SHE opens the bag, takes out
an egg and ham biscuit, puts it in Du's good hand.)* Catsup
already on it. It's an unbelievable steam bath. Not bad in
here. I had a migraine yesterday, but it's on the way out.
So. You have more color. Any luck with the left hand? *(In
a tiny gesture, DU shakes her head "no.")* Well, they said
several months. They were saying you were ahead of
schedule. Your hair looks nice. I just can't get mine done, I
don't know. In this heat. *(SHE picks up the string bag.)*
Let's see. Cranberry juice, tuna packed in water, pretzels,
hot sauce, the hand lotion, eye shadow perfect match. I

couldn't find that mascara, but see what you think. Sorry about yesterday, I just ... new Readers Digest, sequel to *The Clan of the Cave Bear*, peanut butter cremes. The Nyquil. (*To the guard.*) Is that alright? (*GUARD shakes her head "no."*) Stationery. My dear. Something else, but I can't think what.

(*SHE holds up the bag and the GUARD moves forward to take it, and then back to her post.*)

KEELY. Cole gave himself up. You probably heard that. Somewhere in Arizona. Dad had the flu. My God, he's ill-tempered when he's sick. The patient from hell, really. I could throttle him. I may throttle him. (*A pause.*) Every time I come here I come here to forgive you. Why can't I say it? I guess I come here to tell you I'm trying. "God's wrath and God's grace," wasn't that it? I don't seem to have either. (*A moment.*) Oh, there's a new waitress, she wears heels, green contacts, a Bible in her purse and her skirts up to here ... you want to know the truth I think she's into my tips. She brings this dog to work, leaves it in the car, can you believe it, ninety degrees. Oh, I may go on a climb, I don't know, I don't know, the guy is married ... yeah, I know ... Boulder, Colorado the end of the month. Listen, he swears he's separated, plus he's paying. I just should get out, you know? I don't get out. Take my mind off. Anyway. We could talk, you know? I would like that. What do you think? Boiling. So, what are you doing in crafts, that antimacassar stuff? Like you need more, right? (*A pause.*) Any more stealing? (*DU shakes her head "no."*) The ring? (*DU shakes her head "no."*) Boy, it never occurred to me like theft would be a problem in here. Hey, how's the Prozac? They still fooling with the level? (*DU nods "yes."*) Maybe you could slip me some. Joking, you know? So, I went to a Judd concert. You know the one that sings without her mother now … (*SHE stops.*) … without her mother now. I don't know, I left. People, they're about half screwy, you know. People who go to those concerts? There was this guy next to me, he was smoking grass, right out there, had a little girl on his lap, maybe two. (*SHE tears up.*) Had this little girl on his lap. So. I don't know. I don't know. Anyway …

(*The conversation burns out. THEY sit. DU looks directly at her. THEY lock eyes. The pause lengthens.*)

DU. Why?
KEELY. (*Looks at her. A pause.*) Why?

(*THEY sit. The LIGHTS dim.*)

END OF PLAY

COSTUMES

<u>KEELY</u>

Act I

Bikini panties, floral blue/white

White cotton bra (no padding)

Hospital gown blue/white

Act II

Pink maternity panties w/small pad

White padded bra

White flannel nightgown with blue/green flowers

Socks

Dress - teal green long-sleeved knit (pre-set in fridge).
   Change on stage.

Act II, Scene 18

White cotton bra (no padding)

Bikini panties, floral blue/white

Oatmeal color linen dress, button-up center front

Sandals

Necklace - gold chain w/beige & green beads

Gold/green/brown earrings

Hair is up

<u>DU</u>

Act I & II

Pantyhose

White 1/2 slip

White cotton t-shirt

Blue/purple cotton plaid housedress

Dark blue cardigan w/pockets

Beige leather slip-ons

Necklace - cross on chain

Watch
Blue tote purse w/3 pockets
Glasses on chain
Clear plastic 1/2 mask
Act II
Off-white cardigan w/pockets
Act II, Scene 18
White cotton t-shirt
Orange prison zip front jumpsuit
White slip-on sneakers

UNDERLINE WALTER

WALTER
Act I, Scene 1
White V-neck t-shirt
Dark blue pants
White & gray stripe long-sleeved shirt
Light blue sweater
Gray zip front windbreaker
Black loafers
Black socks
Watch
Clear plastic 1/2 mask
Act I, Scenes 5,7,9 & 12
White V-neck t-shirt
White button-down shirt
Gray wool slacks
Same shoes
Same socks
Black belt
Gray, blue & beige stripe tie
Watch

*Change ties for 4 other scenes (tie #2, #3, #4, #5)

Act II, Scene 15
White V-neck t-shirt
White button-down shirt
Dark gray pinstripe suit
Same shoes
Same belt
Watch
Tie #5

COLE
Act II, Scenes 16 & 17
White cotton V-neck t-shirt
White cotton long-sleeved shirt
Dark blue wool suit
Black tie dress shoes
Black socks
Gold band ring
Black belt
Tie

PRISON GUARD
Act II, Scene 18
White cotton V-neck t-shirt
Gray poly shirt w/dark gray pockets with prison patches on
    sleeves
Black poly pants
Black shiny patent leather shoes, tie
Black socks
Black belt
Black snap-to-belt key ring

ORDERLY
Act I, Scene 1
White cotton V-neck t-shirt
Dark green long sleeved polo shirt
Blue jeans
Dark blue windbreaker
Black tennis shoes
Dark blue socks
Braided brown leather belt
Digital watch
Clear plastic full mask

ORDERLY
Act I, Scene 1
White cotton V-neck t-shirt
Blue & white stripe shirt
Tan khaki pants
White cotton w/green lining windbreaker
Brown penny loafers
Brown socks
Brown belt
Digital watch
Clear plastic full mask

ORDERLY (female)
Act I, Scene 1
Button-down shirt
Dark green knit pants
Light blue/gray windbreaker
Blue/green leather flats
Gold cross chain necklace
Black leather watch
Clear plastic full mask

PROPERTY PLOT

Quilt
Pillow
2 sets of sheets
Key pad (to "lock" door; US facing door)
Speaker (on DS facing door)
5 masks (Walter, Du, 3 Orderlies)
Gurney (w/straps to restrain Keely)
Suitcase w/
 Robe
 Toiletry bag
 First aid kit
Slip of paper (w/phone # – Walter to Du)
Note #1 (to Du from hubby: "Love ya, be strong")
Handcuffs (real, total of 5 extra keys)
File of papers (info on Keely, in suitcase)
Water bottle (filled with water, removeable top)
Paper cups
Bucket
Towel
Rag
Tray #1 (cafeteria type) w/
 Fake food
 Cup (separate from tray)
 Spoon
 Napkin
Briefcase (Walter) w/
 Book (Abortion: "The Silent Holocaust" by John
 Powell)
 Bible
 Files

Misc. brochures
Tray #2 (cafeteria style) w/
 Bowl
 Sm. box of cereal
 Spoon
 Napkin
 Milk carton
Paper towels (on fridge)
Grocery bag (paper) w/
 Mouthwash (peppermint)
 Oranges (in plastic bag)
 Emery boards
 Kleenex (sm. box)
 Panties (on small hanger, tags)
 Dr. Spock book
 Two books ("First Year of Life"/Preg book)
 1 really gross pamphlet
Bandage (Keely, slip-on)
Baby shoes (in gift box)
3 photos (of Du's children)
Milkshake (fake w/straw)
Note #2 (from hubby, "hurt but OK")
Tray #3 w/
 Scrambled eggs
 Toast
 Catsup
 Hash browns/home fries
 Cup w/water
 Spoon, fork
 Napkin
Set of sheets, pillow case (Folded, Du changes pillow)
2nd pillow (w/case)

Stethoscope (Du)
Note pad (Du makes note on Keely's health)
Pen
Handkerchief (Walter)
6 abortion pamphlets (tossed off bed)
Key on string (to handcuffs; in Du's purse)
Hanger (from dry-cleaners)
Dry-clean bag (for dress)
Six-pack of beer (discount brand, twist off tops)
Pocket mirror (Du's purse)
Muslin strips (dyed) (to rag Keely's hair; 11, knotted in
    middle)
Comb (Du)
Flower (real, from Cole)
2 blood capsules (taped to Cole's jacket sleeve)
Chair (straight-backed)
Blood (poured on sheet from 2 containers)
Phone (on door, placed over speaker)
Wheel chair
Prison chair
McDonald's sausage/egg biscuit
McDonald's bag
McDonald's wrapper (for biscuit)
McDonald's napkin
String bag (Keely) w/
    Tuna can (packed in water)
    Pretzels
    Hot sauce
    Hand lotion
    Reader's Digest
    Book: "Valley of the Horses"
    Nyquil
    Stationery (in box)

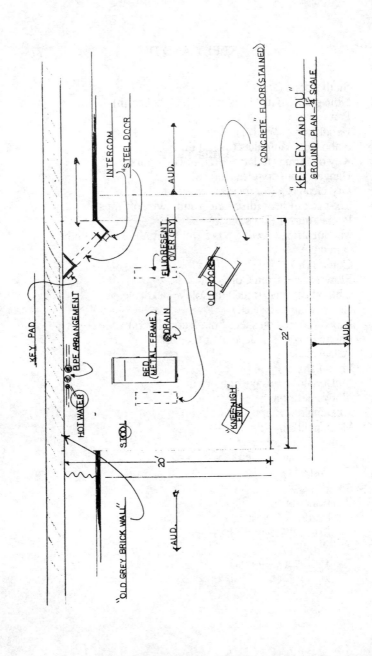

"OLD GREY BRICK WALL"

HOT WATER

STOOL

KEY PAD

PIPE ARRANGEMENT

BED (METAL FRAME)

DRAIN

"KNEE HIGH" FLYS

FLUORESENT OVER (FLY)

OLD ROCKER

INTERCOM

"STEEL DOOR"

"CONCRETE FLOOR(STAINED)"

"KEELEY AND DU"
GROUND PLAN — ¼ SCALE

AUD.

AUD.

AUD.

AUD.

20'

22'

CEMENTVILLE
by Jane Martin
Comedy
Little Theatre

(5m., 9f.) Int. The comic sensation of the 1991 Humana Festival at the famed Actors Theatre of Louisville, this wildly funny new play by the mysterious author of *Talking With* and *Vital Signs* is a brilliant portrayal of America's fascination with fantasy entertainment, "the growth industry of the 90's." We are in a run-down locker room in a seedy sports arena in the Armpit of the Universe, "Cementville, Tennessee," with the scurviest bunch of professional wrasslers you ever saw. This is decidedly a small-time operation—not the big time you see on TV. The promoter, Bigman, also appears in the show. He and his brother Eddie are the only men, though; for the main attraction(s) are the "ladies." There's Tiger, who comes with a big drinking problem and a small dog; Dani, who comes with a large chip on her shoulder against Bigman, who owes all the girls several weeks' pay; Lessa, an ex-Olympic shotputter with delusions that she is actually employed presently in athletics; and Netty, an overweight older woman who appears in the ring dressed in baggy pajamas, with her hair in curlers, as the character "Pajama Mama." There is the eager-beaver go-fer Nola, a teenager who dreams of someday entering the glamorous world of pro wrestling herself. And then, there are the Knockout Sisters, refugees from the Big Time but banned from it for heavy-duty abuse of pharmaceuticals as well as having gotten arrested *in flagrante delicto* with the Mayor of Los Angeles. They have just gotten out of the slammer; but their indefatigable manager, Mother Crocker ("Of the Auto-Repair Crockers") hopes to get them reinstated, if she can keep them off the white powder. Bigman has hired the Knockout Sisters as tonight's main attraction, and the fur really flies along with the sparks when the other women find out about the Knockout Sisters. Bigman has really got his hands full tonight. He's gotta get the girls to tear each other up in the ring, not the locker room; he's gotta deal with tough-as-nails Mother Crocker; he's gotta keep an arena full of tanked-up rubes from tearing up the joint—and he's gotta solve the mystery of who bit off his brother Eddie's dick last night.   (#5580)

XXXXXXXXXXXXXXXXXXXXXXXXXXXX
BURIED TREASURE FROM SAMUEL FRENCH, INC.

Most of the superb plays listed below have never been produced in New York City. Does this mean they aren't "good enough" for New York? JUDGE FOR YOURSELF!

ABOUT FACE -- AN ACT OF THE IMAGINATION -- ALL SHE CARES ABOUT IS THE YANKEES -- ALONE AT THE BEACH -- AMERICAN CANTATA -- THE ANASTASIA FILE -- ARCHANGELS DON'T PLAY PINBALL -- THE BAR OFF MELROSE -- BEDROOMS -- BEYOND REASONABLE DOUBT -- BILL W. AND DR. BOB -- BINGO -- BLUE COLLAR BLUES -- BODYWORK -- BRONTE -- CARELESS LOVE -- CAT'S PAW -- CHEKHOV IN YALTA -- A CHORUS OF DISAPPROVAL -- CINCINNATI -- THE CURATE SHAKESPEARE AS YOU LIKE IT -- DADDY'S DYIN' -- DANCERS -- DARKSIDE -- ELIZABETH -- FIGHTING CHANCE -- FOOLIN' AROUND WITH INFINITY -- GETTING THE GOLD -- GILLETTE -- THE GIRLHOOD OF SHAKESPEARE'S HEROINES -- GOD'S COUNTRY ---- IMAGINARY LINES -- INTERPRETERS -- LLOYD'S PRAYER -- MAKE IN BANGKOK -- MORE FUN THAN BOWLING -- OWNERS -- PAPERS -- PIZZA MAN -- POSTMORTEM -- PRAVDA -- THE PUPPETMASTER OF LODZ - THE REAL QUEEN OF HEARTS AIN'T EVEN PRETTY -- RED NOSES -- RETROFIT -- RETURN ENGAGEMENTS -- THE RIVERS AND RAVINES -- ROBIN HOOD -- SHIVAREE -- A SMALL FAMILY BUSINESS -- STAINED GLASS -- TAKE A PICTURE -- TALES FROM HOLLYWOOD -- TEN NOVEMBER -- THEATER TRIP -- THIS ONE THING I DO -- THIS SAVAGE PARADE -- TRAPS -- THE VOICE OF THE PRAIRIE -- WIDOW'S WEEDS -- THE WISTERIA BUSH -- THE WOMAN IN BLACK

Consult our most recent Catalogue for details.
XXXXXXXXXXXXXXXXXXXXXXXXXXXX